Giraffes

Giraffes

A Carolrhoda Nature Watch Book

by Barbara Keevil Parker

Carolrhoda Books, Inc. / Minneapolis

To Stacy, Roy, Brandon, Makayla—with love

I want to thank Amos D. Morris Jr., former curator at Roger Williams Park Zoo, Providence, RI; Dr. Stanley Aronson, M.D.; Vicki Liestman; and Betty Brown for their assistance with the manuscript. I am grateful to Shannon Zemlicka, whose editorial expertise polished the text. I also want to thank the many authors whose research helped me in writing this text, particularly Andrew Brown, Helen Roney Sattler, Lynn Sherr, Sigmund A. Lavine, Caroline Arnold, Anne Innis Dagg, J. Bristol Foster, and John Bennett Wexo.

The publisher gratefully acknowledges the assistance of Pat Currie, Herbivore/Carnivore Headkeeper, Columbus Zoo; and Fred Barnard, Giraffe Keeper, Miami Metrozoo.

Carolrhoda Books
A division of Lerner Publishing Group
241 First Avenue North
Minneapolis, MN 55401 U.S.A.

Website address: www.lernerbooks.com

Library of Congress Cataloging-in-Publication Data

Parker, Barbara Keevil.
    Giraffes / by Barbara Keevil Parker.
    p.   cm. — (A Carolrhoda nature watch book)
    Summary: Describes the physical characteristics, life cycle, habitat, and behavior of giraffes, as well as efforts to protect them.
    ISBN: 1–57505–346–2 (lib. bdg. : alk. paper)
    1. Giraffe—Juvenile literature. [1. Giraffe.] I. Title. II. Series: Nature watch (Minneapolis, Minn.)
QL737.U56P37 2004
599.638—dc21   2003000008

Manufactured in the United States of America
1 2 3 4 5 6 – JR – 09 08 07 06 05 04

CONTENTS

Opposite page: *A pregnant giraffe awaits the birth of her baby.*
Above: *The African savanna is grassy, flat, and hot.*

A GIANT IS BORN

The midday sun beats hot in East Africa. The sun's rays fall on a grassy plain called a **savanna**. The dry grasses are motionless. The air sits still, heavy with heat. Thorny acacia (uh-KAY-shuh) trees stand silent.

A female giraffe waits. She stands alone on the dry savanna in a place where the grass lies flat. Other animals have grazed and rested here before.

A short distance away, six giraffes graze on the leaves of acacia trees. One of the six watches for danger as they eat. Ever alert, the watcher looks for **predators**—the lion, the hyena, the cheetah—hunters that hide among the grasses. Every few minutes, the watcher turns and looks with soft brown eyes at the waiting female.

The sun climbs higher in the African sky.

At last two small hooves emerge from the female giraffe's birth canal.

The female continues to wait.

A nose and a head follow.

An hour later, a baby giraffe slips from the safety of its mother's body. The **calf** falls headfirst to the ground 6 feet (2 m) below. Thump!

The mother giraffe spreads her legs and lowers her long neck. She licks and washes her baby. She nuzzles him with her nose, encouraging him to stand.

The calf gathers his legs close to his body and tries to get up. Slowly, on wobbly legs, he pushes to stand for the first time. His back legs give way, and he tumbles onto the soft mat of grass. Again the mother giraffe nudges the calf with her nose, urging him to stand.

This time the calf uses his long neck for balance. He throws his neck backwards and gets up on his front knees. Then he swings his neck forward, allowing his hind legs to stretch out and stand. Again he swings his neck backward and struggles to his front feet. He wobbles close to his mother and nuzzles her underbelly, searching for milk. The mother giraffe licks him and leads him away.

Giraffes are the world's tallest mammal. A giraffe is 6.5 feet tall (2.0 m) at birth. By adulthood, it's much bigger.

Picture three tall men standing one on top of the other. Together they *may* equal the height of an adult male giraffe, or **bull**. Bulls reach heights of 18 feet (5.5 m) or more. Females, or **cows**, are 14 to 16 feet (4.3–4.9 m). If your school has classrooms on the second floor, a giraffe could easily look in the window to see what you're studying. If you met a giraffe while riding in the top section of a double-decker bus, you'd discover that the giraffe was a little taller than your seat.

Giraffes are heavy as well as tall. Bulls can weigh as much as 3,000 pounds (1,400 kg), a little more than a medium-sized car. Females weigh 1,500 to 2,600 pounds (680–1,200 kg). These peaceful animals are truly Africa's gentle giants.

Bull giraffes often grow to be 18 feet (5.5 m) tall. The tallest bull ever recorded was 19.3 feet (5.88 m).

9

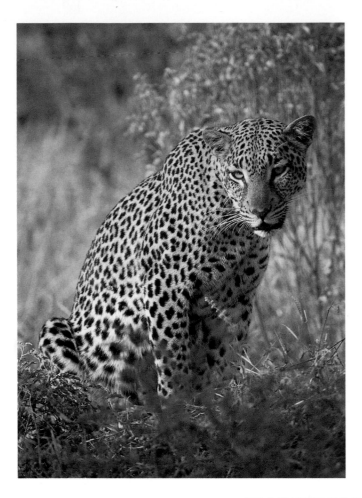

Giraffe spots remind many people of leopard spots.

FAMILY HISTORY

Giraffes belong to a single **species** (SPEE-sheez), or kind, of animal. Members of a species closely resemble each other and can produce young together. The scientific name for the giraffe species is *Giraffa camelopardalis*. How did it get this name?

People of many cultures have noticed that giraffes have spots like a leopard as well as a long neck and two-toed hooves like a camel. An African myth says that God decided to make one last animal. He started with some leftover parts from the leopard and the camel. Then he stretched the creature's neck and legs, and it became the giraffe. The ancient Romans called the giraffe a "camel leopard," thinking it was a cross between the two animals. The ancient Greeks thought the same thing.

The scientist who gave the giraffe its scientific name probably remembered those stories. But giraffes aren't really related to camels or leopards. Scientists sort related animals into groups called families. Giraffes are grouped into the family Giraffidae (jih-RAF-ih-dee). The members of this family are known as giraffids (jih-RAF-ihdz).

Besides the giraffe, the only living giraffid is the okapi (oh-KAH-pee). Okapis live deep in the tropical rain forests of central Africa. They share some traits with giraffes, but they look more like donkeys. Their coat is deep red-brown, and their legs have stripes like a zebra's.

The giraffe's only close living relative is the okapi. Okapis don't look much like giraffes, but the two species have many features in common.

This giraffe's two ossicones are easy to spot between its ears.

All giraffids are **ungulates** (UHNG-yoo-lehts), or hoofed animals. Their hooves are two-toed and shaped like a wedge. Giraffids swallow their food without chewing much and later bring it back into their mouth to chew again. They also have **ossicones**, knobby, horn-like head bumps covered with skin and hair. (Many people call ossicones horns, but true horns aren't covered with skin or hair.)

Human families often keep records of grandparents, great-grandparents, and great-great-grandparents. A family's record is called its family tree. Scientists who study animals also create family trees, records of how a kind of animal has changed over the course of time.

According to scientists, the giraffe family tree began about 20 to 25 million years ago. Ancient giraffes were long-necked animals that lived in Europe, Asia, and Africa. About 1.6 million years ago, the weather grew colder, and many giraffes died out. But in Africa, south of the Sahara Desert, the weather stayed warm enough for giraffes to survive.

Modern giraffes live in the wild only in Africa. Most scientists separate them into nine subspecies. Each subspecies has its own **range**, or living area, though some ranges overlap. Each subspecies also has its own pattern of spots, though some patterns look similar.

This giraffe belongs to the Masai subspecies.

The Nine Giraffe Subspecies

Angolan giraffe
Giraffa camelopardalis angolensis

Kordofan giraffe
Giraffa camelopardalis antiquorum

Masai giraffe
Giraffa camelopardalis tippelskirchi

Nubian giraffe
Giraffa camelopardalis camelopardalis

Reticulated giraffe
Giraffa camelopardalis reticulata

Rothschild's giraffe
Giraffa camelopardalis rothschildi

Southern giraffe
Giraffa camelopardalis giraffa

Thornicroft's giraffe
Giraffa camelopardalis thornicrofti

West African giraffe
Giraffa camelopardalis peralta

Range of Giraffe Subspecies*

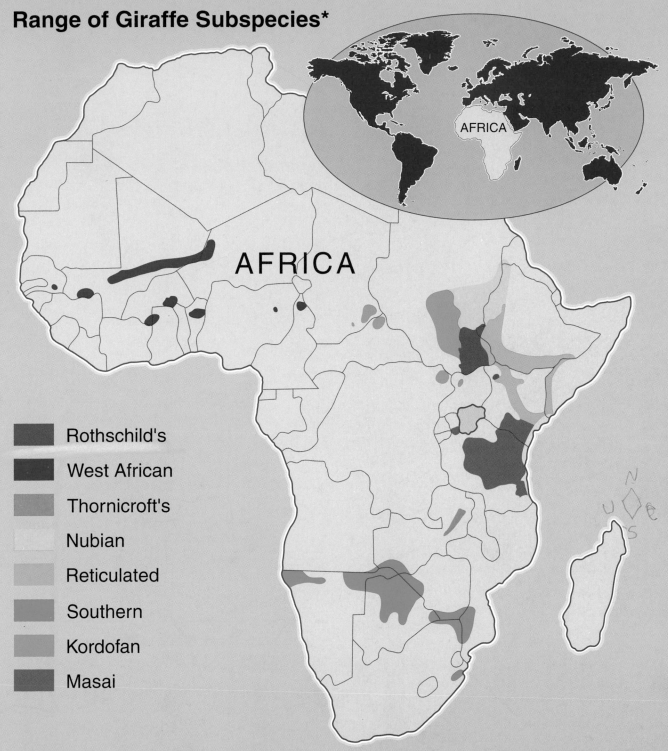

AFRICA

AFRICA

- Rothschild's
- West African
- Thornicroft's
- Nubian
- Reticulated
- Southern
- Kordofan
- Masai

*The Angolan giraffe's range is not shown. It overlaps the western range of the Southern giraffe.

Two Masai giraffes pace across a savanna in Kenya, a country in East Africa.

PHYSICAL CHARACTERISTICS

From tail to head to hooves, the graceful giraffe is an amazing and complex animal. The word *Giraffa* comes from the Arabic word *zirafah* (zee-RAH-fuh). *Zirafah* means "the one that walks very fast." Giraffes can move quickly indeed, running at speeds of up to 35 miles per hour (56 km/hr). A running giraffe pumps its neck back and forth to keep its balance and increase its speed.

Giraffes also have an unusual way of walking, called **pacing**. When a giraffe paces, the front and back left legs move forward at almost the same time, followed by the front and back right legs. Pacing looks slow, but it's rather fast. Very few animals walk by pacing—the okapi and the camel are two examples.

Can you tell which of a giraffe's legs are longer, the front or the back? People often think that a giraffe's front legs are longer than the back legs. But all four legs are nearly equal in length. (The front legs look longer because of the way a giraffe's back slopes.) On a male, the legs alone can be over 6 feet (2 m) long. They end in two-toed hooves that are built to support great weight. The front hooves leave prints the size of a dinner plate!

A giraffe's tail can be as long as 6.6 feet (2.0 m), including the tuft of thick black hair at the end. Each tail hair is thicker than ten strands of your hair put together. Scientists think that giraffes whisk their tails to brush away flies and to warn other giraffes of danger. When running, a giraffe curls its tail over its back, probably to keep the tail away from its legs.

The hairs in a giraffe's tail are about 3 feet (1 m) long.

One third of a giraffe's height is made up of its neck and head. The neck alone can be 5.0 to 6.5 feet (1.5–2.0 m) long. It's made up of strong muscles as well as bones called **vertebrae** (VUR-tuh-bray), which support the neck the way a frame supports a building.

A giraffe's neck has seven vertebrae. That's the same number that humans and most other mammals have in their neck. How can such a long neck contain the same number of bones as a person's short neck? The size of the bones makes the difference. Each of a giraffe's neck vertebrae can be 11 inches (28 cm) long. A human's neck vertebrae are less than 2 inches (5 cm) long.

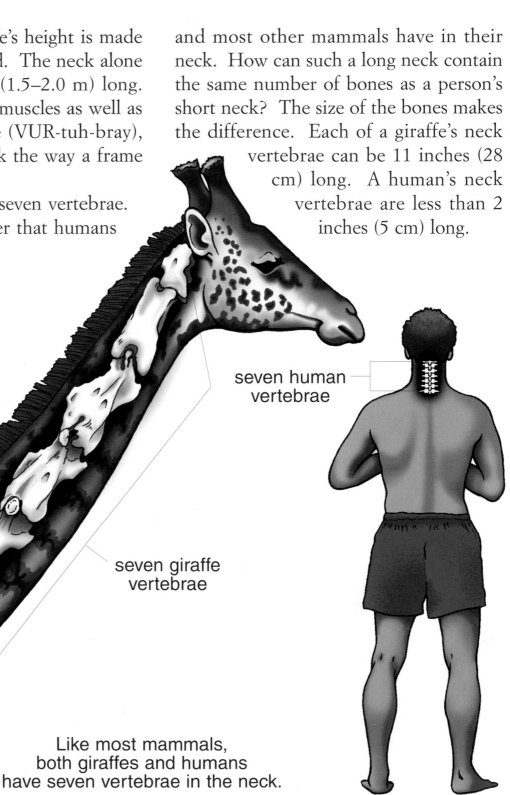

seven human vertebrae

seven giraffe vertebrae

Like most mammals, both giraffes and humans have seven vertebrae in the neck.

The hornlike ossicones that top a bull giraffe's head can be 9 inches (20 cm) long and 6 inches (15 cm) around. A cow's ossicones are shorter and thinner. Many giraffes, especially bulls, grow a large, hair-covered bump on the forehead called a **median horn**. Some giraffe subspecies grow two additional ossicones behind their ears, giving them five in all.

Giraffes are **herbivores** (UR-bih-vohrz), or plant eaters. They eat seedpods, fruits, twigs, and leaves from trees and shrubs. Giraffes have several features that help them eat. A giraffe's upper lip is hairy and **prehensile** (pree-HEN-suhl), which means it can bend to grasp objects like a finger can. The prehensile lip can easily wrap around branches and leaves.

A giraffe's prehensile lip helps it grasp leaves and branches.

A joint at the base of the neck allows a giraffe to bend the neck straight up to reach high plants. A giraffe's long tongue extends its reach even farther.

A giraffe's dark, purplish-black tongue is 1.5 feet (0.46 m) long. Like the upper lip, the tongue is prehensile. It can extend far out of the giraffe's mouth to wrap around plants that the upper lip can't reach.

If you were to stick your fingers inside a giraffe's mouth, you'd discover that it has front teeth only on the bottom jaw. These teeth work with the upper lip to comb leaves from branches. Back teeth are used for chewing.

20

Giraffes don't do much chewing as they eat. Instead, they swallow their food quickly. Later, when they're resting, they bring a small amount of food back up the throat and into the mouth. This blob of food is about the size of a baseball and is called a **cud**. A giraffe chews its cud completely and swallows it again. This way of eating is called **ruminating**. Animals that ruminate, such as giraffes, cows, and bison, are called ruminants.

Ruminants have several chambers in their stomach—usually four. Each chamber plays a different role in processing food. Why do ruminants need to chew cud and send it through four stomach chambers? The plants they eat are hard for the body to digest, or break down to remove nutrients. Extra chewing and the stomach's several chambers help ruminants get as much nutrition from their food as possible.

A giraffe chews its cud to make it easier to digest.

Like all mammals, a giraffe relies on its heart to move blood throughout its body. The blood travels through narrow tubes called blood vessels, carrying oxygen and food. A giraffe's heart has a big job to do. It pumps blood all the way up to the head and all the way down to the feet—20 gallons (80 l.) per minute! That's enough to fill a small fish tank. The heart is big enough to handle all this pumping. It weighs 25 pounds (11 kg) and measures 2 feet (0.6 m) long.

Picture a giraffe lowering its head to drink. Why doesn't a huge amount of blood flow down into the brain? The blood vessels in a giraffe's neck have special valves. The valves close when the giraffe lowers its head. As a dam stops a river from flowing, the valves stop blood from rushing down the neck. Giraffes also have valves that keep too much blood from flowing into the feet.

Strong senses help giraffes stay safe. They have excellent vision. They can spot a predator 1 mile (2 km) away, giving them plenty of time to run for safety. Giraffes also hear very well. Their ears are 8 inches (20 cm) long. When a group of giraffes hears an unfamiliar sound, every member of the group turns toward the noise to listen. Their ears move in the direction of the noise.

Giraffes move their long ears in the direction of the sounds they hear.

Spots help this Masai mother and calf blend into the background.

Another characteristic that helps giraffes stay safe is their spots. Almost all giraffes have spots, though occasionally one is born without any. Spot patterns are pretty, but they're not for looks. They make giraffes hard for predators to see against the savanna's plants, ground, sunlight, and shadows. Like the multicolored uniforms that soldiers wear, spots **camouflage** (KAM-uh-flahzh) a giraffe by blending with the background.

Spots serve a purpose for scientists, too. No two giraffes have the same pattern of spots. Scientists use the patterns on giraffe necks to tell one giraffe from another. By photographing necks, scientists can create a catalog of all the giraffes they're studying. When they spot an individual giraffe, they simply match a photograph with the giraffe's neck to identify it.

A herd of reticulated giraffes in Kenya

HERD LIFE AND DAILY ROUTINE

Giraffes spend much of their time in groups called **herds**. A herd of animals eats, sleeps, and travels together. Giraffe herds have 12 to 15 members. A single herd may be made up of bulls only, both bulls and cows, or cows and calves.

Members of a giraffe herd don't usually form close bonds with each other. In fact, a herd's membership changes constantly as giraffes come and go. The longest-lasting bonds among giraffes are between mothers and their calves.

Living in herds has helped giraffes survive for millions of years. Giraffe herds are constantly on the lookout for enemies. Their long necks serve as lookout towers. Many other animals, such as zebras, wildebeests, and ostriches, graze near giraffes. These animals seem to feel safe knowing that the giraffes are keeping watch.

Lions and humans are the main enemies of the giraffe. They are the only predators that hunt full-grown giraffes. If a giraffe spots one of these enemies, it alerts the other members of the herd. A startled giraffe holds its head straight up, flares its nostrils, spreads its ears stiffly, holds its body motionless, and stares with eyes blazing. It paws the ground or switches its tail rapidly from side to side as a danger signal to other giraffes. Sometimes it snorts, too.

Giraffes are peaceful animals. They would rather run from danger than fight. An alarmed giraffe usually gallops away, followed by the other giraffes in the herd. But if a giraffe has no other choice, it will protect itself and its young by kicking its legs. A single giraffe kick can kill a lion.

What do you think has startled this reticulated giraffe?

Giraffes communicate with other sounds besides snorting. Sometimes cow giraffes make a mooing noise or whistle to call their young. A calf that's in trouble or lonely will bleat, making a soft cry like a sheep's. Giraffes also grunt, cough, growl, and snore. But most of the time, they don't make a sound. Body language is their most important means of communication.

Male giraffes spend less time in herds than females. When males become adults, they often live alone. At times they travel from herd to herd, hoping to find a female with which to mate. Sometimes they form herds with other bulls.

From the time they are young, male giraffes engage in **necking**. Necking giraffes rub their head and neck against one another. When bulls get older, necking shifts to a fight to show which bull is the strongest. Two bulls who are about to fight stand together. Each holds his head high, which is a threatening gesture. One giraffe swings his neck and head like a baseball bat, smashing against the other giraffe's neck or shoulder. The bulls poke at each other with their ossicones, too.

Most of the time, neither giraffe is hurt. Ossicones usually don't do much damage, but bulls also crash heads. A bull's skull can be as long as 2 feet (6 m) and weighs about 22 pounds (10 kg). The impact of two crashing heads can cause broken jaws and necks.

The fighters pound against each other until one bull walks or runs away. The winner of the fight becomes the herd's **dominant** (DAH-mih-nehnt) male. He gets the first choice of food to eat and females for mates. Once the bulls have determined which one is dominant, they live together peacefully, rubbing necks and eating.

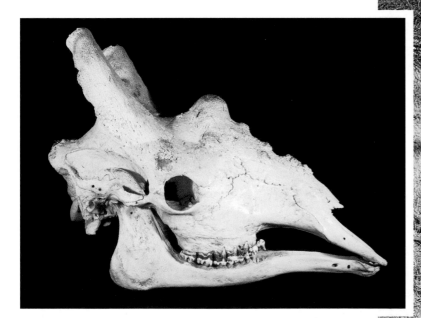

Above: *The thick, bony skull of a bull giraffe*
Right: *Two reticulated bulls fight to determine which is the most powerful.*

Thorns don't stop a giraffe from eating acacia branches.

Whether they're in herds or alone, giraffes spend much of their time eating. Cows spend about 13 hours a day eating, while bulls eat for 10 hours. During that time, a giraffe munches about 75 pounds (34 kg) of plants, usually tree leaves.

Giraffes eat by **browsing**. A browsing giraffe wraps its prehensile upper lip around a branch and rakes off the leaves with its prehensile tongue. The giraffe spends a short time at each tree, picking the freshest and most tender growth. It eats from the highest point it can reach down to 4 feet (about 1 m) above the ground. The tree's lower leaves are left behind. Other, smaller animals eat them.

Acacia leaves are the favorite food of giraffes. The branches of acacia trees have thorns and sometimes ants. But thorns and ants don't stop a hungry giraffe. It eats thorns, ants, and all.

Along with food, giraffes need water to live. They get most of the water they need from the plants they eat. Acacia twigs are more than two-thirds water, for example. But giraffes have been known to drink 2 gallons (8 l.) in a typical week and as much as 10 gallons (40 l.) on a hot day. During droughts—long periods without rain—giraffes can go without drinking water for up to 8 days. Some scientists think they could survive without water for several months.

When a giraffe is standing, its neck isn't long enough to reach water on the ground. But giraffes cannot wade into a water hole to drink, either. They cannot swim, and because they are so heavy, they could get stuck in the mud. So a thirsty giraffe must spread its front legs wide apart to get closer to the ground. Then its neck can bend low enough to reach water. In this position, the giraffe may not see other animals approaching. If the giraffe is alone, it could be attacked by a lion or another predator.

A lion attacks a giraffe by leaping on the giraffe's neck. If the lion's weight pushes the giraffe to the ground, the giraffe becomes helpless. The lion will quickly kill it by breaking its neck or strangling it with strong jaws. Crocodiles also kill young giraffes at water holes. For safety, giraffes usually visit water holes in groups. One giraffe watches for danger while the others drink.

One giraffe keeps watch while another bends low to drink.

A Masai giraffe scratches itself with its teeth.

Giraffes also face danger when eating salt, which they must have to stay healthy. They get salt from salt licks, places where salt is found naturally in the earth. Just as they must to reach water, giraffes must spread their front legs wide apart to reach salt. Again, one giraffe usually watches for danger while others eat the salty earth.

Living in herds helps giraffes keep clean as well as safe. Giraffes never bathe. Instead, they occasionally clean themselves by licking with their long tongue. They lick others in the herd, too. They also use their tongue to clean their ears and nostrils.

To get rid of dirt and to scratch itchy spots, a giraffe nibbles its body with its lower teeth. Its long neck allows it to reach along its back all the way to the tail. Giraffes also rub their necks against tree trunks and scratch their heads against branches. To ease an itching belly, a giraffe straddles a thorny bush or a termite mound and wiggles back and forth.

Birds called oxpeckers help giraffes with their cleaning by hitching a ride on them. Oxpeckers climb over a giraffe's body in search of fleas, other insects, and ticks to eat. The birds get a meal, and the giraffe is rid of pests that spread disease and cause itching. Sometimes oxpeckers peck at sores on a giraffe's body. The giraffe may not like how this feels, but the pecking removes disease-spreading maggots from the sore area.

Giraffes spend most of their time browsing and chewing their cud. When do they sleep? During the day, adult giraffes sometimes doze off, but never for more than a few minutes. A dozing giraffe usually remains standing. With its neck drooping, tail still, and eyelids low, it rests.

Oxpeckers clean giraffes by eating pests that live on their body.

At night, giraffes lie down to sleep for short periods. To lie down, a giraffe folds its front legs under its body, then bends its back legs. Adult giraffes hold their head erect or rest it on their rump or a hind leg. Calves curl up on the ground with their neck tucked back over their rump. Giraffes usually don't sleep lying down for longer than 3 to 4 minutes.

Then they wake to check for danger.

Getting up is more work than lying down. First the giraffe raises its front legs slightly. Then it raises the back legs, and then the front legs again. Swinging its long neck back and forth helps the giraffe balance as it stands. In this way, it sleeps and wakes until morning brings back browsing time again.

A reticulated giraffe takes a rare daytime rest.

A bull sniffs and tastes a cow's urine to find out if she is ready to mate.

LIFE CYCLE

A female giraffe is ready to mate by the time she is 4 years old. Bulls may be ready to mate at 4 to 5 years, but they usually don't mate until they are 7 or 8 years old. It usually takes a bull a few years to become strong enough to defeat other bulls in necking contests. Until then, he probably can't win a mate.

Bulls know when it's time to mate by sniffing and tasting a cow's urine, which changes as her body gets ready to become pregnant. If a bull takes interest in mating with a certain cow, he courts her by following closely behind her. When she stops, the bull raises a front leg and taps it against the cow's hind leg. Or he may rest his head against her flank. If the cow doesn't move, she is ready to mate. Once the giraffes have mated, the bull leaves. The cow will raise the calf on her own.

Can you imagine a newborn baby that stands 6.5 feet (2.0 m) tall and weighs 120 to 150 pounds (54–68 kg)? That's the size of a newborn giraffe. A human baby is small by comparison—it weighs just 6 to 10 pounds (3–5 kg) and measures about 1.8 feet (0.54 m) long.

A mother Masai giraffe grooms her 3-day-old newborn.

To reach such a big size, a calf grows in its mother's womb for about 15 months. That means a cow is usually 5 years old when her first calf is born. She will have about 10 calves over the course of her lifetime.

When it's time to give birth, a mother giraffe goes off by herself. She stands while the calf is born. Usually only one giraffe is born at a time, but sometimes a cow has twins. The calf drops headfirst, 6 feet (2 m) to the ground. The baby's fall doesn't hurt it. Along with the mother giraffe's licking, the drop to the ground helps to start the calf's breathing.

After a calf is born, it rests on the ground for a few minutes, then tries to stand. Standing isn't easy—it can take from 30 to 60 minutes for the calf to get all the way to its feet. But standing is very important for safety. The mother is anxious to move her baby away from the birth area. The smell of blood from the birth draws predators such as lions and hyenas. If the weak newborn lingers too long, it may be attacked.

A few minutes after the mother and calf leave the birth area, the calf drinks its mother's milk from the **teats**, or nipples, between her back legs. The calf will continue to drink milk from its mother for 9 to 10 months. It will also start to nibble on leaves when it is 6 weeks old.

For the first 2 days of the calf's life, the mother giraffe noses it constantly, encouraging it to follow her. Then the calf learns its mother's scent and starts to follow her on its own. For a week or so, the mother usually keeps her calf with her, away from the rest of the herd.

When the calf is 3 to 4 weeks old, the mother takes it to the herd's nursery, which is called a **crèche** (KREHSH). Here one or more adult cows watch over a few calves. This baby-sitting allows mother giraffes to wander away to browse. In the nursery, calves play together by running, bucking, and rubbing necks.

A reticulated calf drinks milk from its mother's teats.

36

A young giraffe's hair is soft and slightly woolly. Giraffes are born with their spots, but the spots are lighter in color than those of older giraffes. The spots may change shape and will darken as the calf grows older.

Giraffes are born with their ossicones. Tassels of dark hair on a calf's head mark the ossicones' location. The hair covers tiny lumps of strong, flexible tissue called **cartilage** (KAR-tih-lihj). At first, ossicones are just these tiny lumps. Over time, the ossicones grow, and the cartilage hardens into bone. The ossicones reach their full size after a few years.

Opposite page: *This young giraffe's mother watches closely to make sure it is safe.*
Right: *Over time, the spots on this reticulated calf will darken to the same color as its mother's spots.*

This calf has grown almost as tall as its mother's back.

Calves grow quickly. They grow about 3 inches (8 cm) a month and 3 feet (1 m) in their first year. Giraffes keep growing until they are 7 or 8.

As the young giraffes grow, they remain with their mothers in a herd. Cows and calves get along well. Cows often groom each other's calves. Mothers allow other cows' calves to drink milk from their teats, too. But only a mother and her own calf are truly close.

Even with the help of its mother and the herd, many dangers threaten a giraffe calf. Predators rarely kill adult giraffes. But young giraffes aren't as lucky. If a mother leaves a calf alone, even for a short time, a predator may find and kill it. Leopards, lions, crocodiles, cheetahs, and hyenas attack calves and old, lame adult giraffes.

Giraffes have other natural enemies. **Parasites** are living things that live on or inside other living things. Tapeworms and ticks are parasites that attack giraffes, often damaging their health. A disease called rinderpest has shortened the lives of many giraffes. Out of every four calves, predators and diseases claim the lives of two or three during the first year.

If a calf survives its first year, it could live a long life. A healthy giraffe in the wild often lives 15 to 20 years. Some live to be 25 years old. In a zoo, one giraffe survived to the age of 37. Unfortunately, another predator—human beings—has made it difficult for most giraffes to survive that long.

The young giraffe on the left is almost full grown.

39

Cave-dwelling humans painted these giraffes thousands of years ago in North Africa.

GIRAFFES AND PEOPLE

People have lived near giraffes for thousands of years. Some African cave paintings of giraffes are 5,000 years old. Ancient Egyptians decorated pottery and ax handles with images of giraffes. Egyptian rulers put giraffes in parades and gave them as gifts to leaders of other countries.

For thousands of years, African hunters killed giraffes only for food and for their thick but lightweight hides. Hides were used to make sandals, boots, buckets, shields, and drums. Giraffe tails became bracelets and flyswatters. Bones were used for buttons or added to soil to help crops grow.

Then, in the 1400s, people came to Africa from Europe to make settlements, explore, and hunt. Unlike the Africans, the Europeans had guns for hunting. Over the next few hundred years, they killed thousands of giraffes. Like the Africans, European settlers used giraffe meat and hides. But they also killed giraffes for sport. And they gave guns to Africans, who killed more giraffes.

This overhunting nearly wiped out giraffes for good. Then, in the early 1900s, people became concerned about the disappearing giraffe. In 1933, laws were passed to create national parks and game reserves where giraffes and other animals are protected from hunting. Each country where giraffes live also has its own laws about giraffe hunting.

Giraffes are no longer in danger of becoming **extinct**, or dying out forever. But even in protected areas, **poachers**—hunters who kill animals illegally—continue to kill giraffes. Africa's human population is growing quickly. In many places, people are hungry and poor. People who have little to eat are willing to risk killing a forbidden animal to put food on their table. Poachers sell giraffe meat for food. Hides and tails are sold to people who make jewelry and other trinkets for tourists to buy.

This Masai giraffe lives in Serengeti National Park, where animals are protected from hunting.

These Masai giraffes live near a road used by people. Giraffes are sometimes killed by cars and trucks.

Another problem is that giraffes and people are competing for the same land. People need land to grow food. As the African population grows, more of the land where giraffes live and browse is being turned into farmland. That means less food and less living space for giraffes.

Giraffes usually don't bother people or the livestock and crops they raise. Some people allow giraffes to browse on their cattle ranches. Giraffes keep acacia trees trimmed, causing more grass to grow. That means there's more grass for cattle to eat. But the invasion of people has also brought new hazards for giraffes. They can be caught in telephone wires or electrical wires. Sometimes cars or trains hit them.

The Rothschild's giraffe almost died out forever in the 1970s. People saved the subspecies by moving animals to national parks.

The Rothschild's giraffe is an example of a subspecies that was in danger of becoming extinct in the 1970s. Too much of its living space was developed into farmland. Fortunately, people were able to move some Rothschild's giraffes to national parks where the giraffes had more space. These moves helped save the subspecies from being lost.

Giraffes no longer wander throughout most of Africa, as they once did. As the human population continues to grow, the time may come when giraffes exist only in national parks. With limited space, their numbers will drop.

The good news is that many people are working to help giraffes. A group called the African Wildlife Foundation works with communities to help people earn a living without harming wild animals. The Wildlife Clubs of Kenya teach children how to treat land and animals wisely and respectfully.

Governments are trying to help, too. Tourism is becoming one of the most important sources of income in many African countries. Tourists want to see wildlife, so governments are working harder to save giraffes and other animals.

Children meet a Rothschild's giraffe at an educational center in Kenya where giraffes are protected.

How can we help the giraffe? If people stop buying giraffe products such as jewelry made from giraffe tails, poachers will stop killing giraffes to make these things. If we support organizations that protect wilderness, additional land can be set aside for giraffes' living space. And if we support organizations that help hungry people, perhaps fewer giraffes will be killed for food. Hopefully there will never be a day when giraffes are gone from the world.

Most of us will never have the chance to travel to Africa to see giraffes as they are—wild yet gentle, curious yet shy. Most people will never see that wild giraffes are graceful, stately, and willing to share their home with visitors. But we can visit giraffes in zoos around the world. May the hauntingly beautiful eyes of the giraffe continue to thrill those who take time to look.

GLOSSARY

browsing: grazing on leaves and other plants

bull: an adult male giraffe

calf: a young giraffe

camouflage: to hide by blending in with the background

cartilage: strong, flexible tissue that makes up a young giraffe's ossicones

cows: adult female giraffes

crèche: a nursery where adult female giraffes watch over young giraffes

cud: food brought up from a giraffe's stomach to be chewed a second time

dominant: strongest in a group of animals

extinct: died out forever

herbivores: animals that eat plants

herds: groups of giraffes that live, eat, and travel together

median horn: a skin-covered bump in the middle of a giraffe's forehead

necking: neck rubbing and head crashing by male giraffes

ossicones: skin-covered nubs of bone on the head, similar to horns

pacing: a giraffe's way of walking quickly

parasites: living things that live on or inside other living things, often damaging them

poachers: people who kill animals illegally

predators: animals that kill and eat other animals

prehensile: able to bend and grasp objects

range: the area in which a type of animal or plant lives

ruminating: eating by chewing food a second time after it is brought back to the mouth from the stomach

savanna: a flat, grassy plain

species: a kind of animal or plant

teats: nipples

ungulates: hoofed animals

vertebrae: bones that support and give shape to the neck and back

INDEX

ABOUT THE AUTHOR

Barbara Keevil Parker enjoys observing animals while hiking at Mount Rainier National Park and at her home in Everett, Washington. Her love of giraffes has taken her to zoos and wildlife centers around the United States. Ms. Parker is the author of another Carolrhoda Nature Watch book, *North American Wolves,* as well as books about Susan B. Anthony and Miguel de Cervantes. She is a member of the Society of Children's Book Writers and Illustrators and an instructor at the Institute of Children's Literature.

PHOTO ACKNOWLEDGMENTS

The photographs in this book appear courtesy of: © Michele Burgess, pp. 2, 6, 7, 9, 10, 16, 17, 19, 21, 23, 24, 25, 30, 32, 34, 36, 38, 41, 42, 43, 44, 45; © Joe McDonald/Visuals Unlimited, pp. 4–5, 8, 12, 26, 27 (right), 28, 35; © Ken Lucas/Visuals Unlimited, pp. 11, 27 (left); © John Gerlach/Visuals Unlimited, p. 13; © Dennis Drenner/Visuals Unlimited, p. 20; © Rob & Ann Simpson/Visuals Unlimited, p. 22; © Don Fawcett/Visuals Unlimited, p. 29; © Gerald & Buff Corsi/Visuals Unlimited, p. 31; © G. L. E./Visuals Unlimited, p. 33; © William J. Weber/Visuals Unlimited, p. 37; PhotoDisc Royalty Free, p. 39; Archivo Iconografico, S.A./CORBIS, p. 40. Cover photo © Michele Burgess.